To: Jessica

From: Mommy & Daddy - June 10, 1999
Kindergarden
Graduation

Published by Garborg's Heart 'n Home, Inc., P.O. Box 20132, Bloomington, MN 55420

ISBN 1-881830-57-8

The ABCs of Friendship

A friend loves at all times.

PROVERBS 17:17 NIV

A friend is what the heart needs all the time.

HENRY VAN DYKE

Blessed are the ones God sends to show
His love for us...our friends.

Chance introduced us,
Hearts made us friends.

Caring and loving build friendships that last.

Doubling our joys and dividing our sorrows,
Our friendship will deepen through
all our tomorrows.

Everyone was meant to share God's
all-abiding love and care; He saw that we
would need to know a way to let these
feelings show. So God made hugs.

JILL WOLF

Encourage each other to build each other up.

1 THESSALONIANS 5:11 TLB

Friends...they cherish each other's hopes.
They are kind to each other's dreams.

HENRY DAVID THOREAU

Good company on a journey makes the way
to seem the shorter.

IZAAK WALTON

How good it feels, the hand of an old friend!

HENRY WADSWORTH LONGFELLOW

I always thank God for you.

PHILIPPIANS 1:3 NIV

I said a prayer for you today...
I asked for happiness...
In all things great and small.
But it was God's loving care
I prayed for most of all.

Just the presence of a caring friend
can make a world of difference.

SHERI CURRY

Kindness and thoughtfulness are two
of the most wonderful ways you
share yourself with me!

Laughter and the love of
friends carry us far to
undiscovered ends.

Life wouldn't be the same without
you and all the memories
you've given me.

May you always find three welcomes in life,
In a garden during summer,
At a fireside during winter,
And whatever the day or season,
In the kind eyes of a friend.

Now may the warming love of friends
surround you as you go
Down the path of light and laughter
where the happy memories grow.

HELEN LOWRIE MARSHALL

Our lives are filled with simple joys
and blessings without end,
And one of the greatest joys in life
is to have a friend.

Perhaps you'd be a bit surprised
how often, if you knew,
A joke, a song, a memory
will make me think of you.

Quiet gratitude fills my heart when I thank
God for the friend I've found in you.

Recall it as often as you wish,
a happy memory never wears out.

LIBBIE FUDIM

Sharing openly, laughing often,
trusting always, and caring deeply—
this is friendship.

Something that is stronger and deeper
than any words is found
in friendship.

Threads of friendship embroider our lives with patterns of joy.

Until we meet again, may God hold you
in the palm of His hand.

Volumes have been written about friendship
but mere words can't describe the sweetness
of your spirit, the warmth of your smile,
and the comfort of your presence.

We are each a secret to the other.

ALBERT SCHWEITZER

When hands reach out in friendship,
hearts are touched with joy.

"Xtra" special closeness and understanding are
part of the magic of our friendship.

You're my friend—
What a thing friendship is, world without end!

ROBERT BROWNING

Zany laughter, unexpected tears, and our easy
openness fashion the unique and colorful
pattern of our friendship.